Textbook

Of

The Tarot

By Janet Berres

International Tarot Society, Inc.
P.O. Box 1475
Morton Grove, IL 60053

First Printing 1993
Second Revised Edition 1997

Foreword

This book has evolved from a one page typed hand-out done 18 years ago to what you're about to read. It has been added to, revised, corrected and rewritten and still may be again because the Tarot cards are not a static discipline but rather a living symbolic art form that fluctuates and breathes and grows. This book is meant as a jumping off point for you to question, analyze and develop your own system that works for you.

I would like to thank Ellen Locatelli, at TekType, Inc. for her beautiful typesetting; she is truly the Magician with her craft. I'd like to thank my sons, Ben and Dan for being as patient as two young boys can be while I was studying and reading the cards (and who have become two great young men). I'd also like to thank my mom and dad, Roslyn and Larry Zukernick and sister Bird (Roberta) Rubinson who were supportive in hard times, and other friends too numerous to mention (you know who you are!).

Table of Contents

Introduction

The Major Arcana 1

The Minor Arcana 25
    Wands. 26
    Cups. 40
    Swords 54
    Pentacles 68

The Spreads 84
    Celtic Cross. 88
    Astrology. 89
    Health. 90
    Tree of Life 91
    Pyramid 92
    3-Month 93

Numbers and the Cards. 94

Colors and the Cards. 96

Symbols in the Cards. 98

Introduction

The Tarot cards are 78 pictured cards that were the forerunners of our modern playing cards. The "average" deck is divided into 22 Major Arcana cards and 56 Minor Arcana cards. (I say average because some decks now have as many as 100 cards or as few as 56, but most have the 78.) The word "arcana" is the plural of the word arcanum which simply means that which is hidden or secret; therefore there are 22 major secrets and 56 minor secrets.

In this book I will be using the Waite/Rider deck which is probably the most widely used deck in existence today. It is called one or both names because of Arthur Edward Waite who was the designer, and Rider Co. who was the publisher. Unfortunately, the artist, Pamela Coleman Smith, was not acknowledged.

The Major Arcana cards tell the big, mostly psychological changes a person is going through. They carry more influence than the Minor Arcana cards which usually depict people and specific events. When a preponderance of Major Arcana appears in a spread, it denotes that things may be out of the querent's (person asking the questions) control.

The Minor Arcana is divided into 4 suits of 14 cards each, numbered one through 10, with each suit having a page, knight, queen and king. In our modern playing cards, the Major Arcana were eliminated except for the Fool who became the Joker, and the page and knight combined to become the jack, leaving each suit with 13 cards. Thus were the decks of today (which consist of 52 cards) created.

As for the history of the Tarot, nobody really knows where the cards originated. Before the invention of the printing press they were hand painted for the nobility of various European countries, but they existed prior to that time. For further information on the history of the Tarot, check out *The Encyclopedia of The Tarot* by Stuart Kaplan, *Tarot Symbolism* by Robert V. O'Neill, or Cynthia Giles' *Tarot: History, Mystery and Lore.*

There are several misconceptions about the cards I would like to clear up now. One of them is that you must keep your deck wrapped in silk, or in an oak box. Actually both of these ideas are nice, but not absolutely necessary. If it makes you feel good to wrap your cards and/or keep them in a wooden box, by all means do so, but only if you choose to. Another misconception which I've also seen in books is that you should sleep with the cards under your pillow at night. To that I say, either you'll wake up in the morning with a headache or have to play "78 pick-up" around the bed the next day. Again, if you want to sleep with the cards under your pillow, fine, but don't feel it's mandatory. And, lastly, although most people feel you have to be "psychic" to read the cards, I believe everyone is psychic and we just develop it or don't develop it to a certain degree. It's a talent, like playing the piano. The more you practice, the better you get! The cards are a wonderful tool to use to help develop your intuition and to learn to trust your hunches and feelings. Someone who dresses in black and wears all sorts of strange jewelry doesn't necessarily have more psychic ability than you. (If you want to dress strangely and wear a lot of jewelry, that's fine too.) Either way, the psychic feelings are in us all, waiting to be tapped.

In reading the cards it is important to feel relaxed and calm. You *can* read the cards under stress but you really must be very disciplined to do so. The pictures presented to you should tell a story and sometimes the cards that don't show up are as important as the ones that do. If a person asks a question about romance, for example, and the suit of Cups is absent, it tells me that the emotional involvement is lacking, even though the relationship could be good in other ways.

Now you are ready to lay the cards out and do the reading. In doing a reading you must first learn the cards, then learn the spreads, and finally you must learn how to synthesize the two. Please read through the definitions of the cards which follows. There will be several different and varied definitions for each card. Not all definitions will apply—usually only one will. It is up to you (the reader) to use discretion (or your psychic feeling) to decide which meaning to use. The picture in the card should show you exactly what the card means, so study the pictures carefully. You may want to make notations in the book because a card may have a meaning for you which I've not even touched upon.

Think of the cards as a road map, you as the tour guide, and the querent as the tourist on the road of life.

Enjoy the journey!

The

Major

Arcana

0

The Fool

PLANET: URANUS
KEY WORDS: FREEDOM;
THE UNEXPECTED

When the Fool card shows up in a reading, the querent (person inquiring) will gain a new outlook on life. It also indicates the beginning of a new cycle in life. This card represents optimism and joy, but also can mean that caution is needed. In the card's picture, the young man is about to walk off of a cliff and is not watching where he is going. Carelessness could be a result and this can mean that more attention to details is needed. A naive outlook can be implied. The Fool card can also represent a spontaneous and carefree attitude and a person who is a dreamer or childlike. While the Fool can mean the querent is beginning anew and will be starting out fresh and optimistically, if the cards around the Fool look bad, the querent may be impulsive and lack good judgement with his "head in the clouds." New experiences will broaden one's horizons, and new people come with these new experiences. Can the Fool mean falling in love? Definitely Yes. One just shouldn't leap without looking or having a net underneath!

THE MAGICIAN.

I

The Magician

PLANET: MERCURY
KEY WORDS: INTELLECT;
MANUAL DEXTERITY; CONTROL

When the Magician shows up, the querent will be taking control of his life and organizing his home, office, etc. The querent feels as though he can change anything. The position of the Magician's hands indicate "as above, so below." Therefore it signifies an attunement with the universe, or harnessing universal forces. This is the card of the doctor or healer. A talent for metaphysics through mental training and will power is indicated; yoga, karate, numerology and the I Ching would be examples. The Magician represents the conscious mind. Symbolically the Magician represents the youthful, active side of men. Also, this card shows one who has skill and manual dexterity as seen by the slight-of-the-hand Magician, which is drawn in the decks of the late 1800's (for example, the Swiss deck). There is a feeling of being captain of one's ship and in control of one's destiny with this card.

THE HIGH PRIESTESS

II

The High Priestess

PLANET: MOON
KEY WORDS: INTUITION;
INNER REFLECTION

T he High Priestess card indicates that the person should follow his instincts and hunches, for they will be correct. A strong psychic ability is shown, with emphasis on Tarot cards, mediumship, automatic writing, crystal gazing and palmistry (all of the *intuitive* arts). Things that are mysterious or hidden appear fascinating. Dreams, omens and symbols may become important now. And because the High Priestess is seated before a veil, she is the keeper of the mysteries yet to be revealed. She represents the unconscious mind, intuition and spiritual insights. Symbolically, the High Priestess shows the virginal, maidenly side of women.

III

The Empress

PLANET: VENUS
KEY WORDS: HARMONY;
BEAUTY; WOMEN

T he Empress card can indicate fertility, pregnancy or creative growth in other ways. This card also represents an interest in the home and luxury for the querent. It is a time to indulge and pamper oneself. The person could be decorating his living quarters or entertaining in the home. The Empress also can indicate new clothes as an effort to beautify oneself. Material comfort is indicated, and sometimes this card represents a woman who is a homemaker and does not work outside of the home; this card can also represent a fair haired woman. The Empress symbolically shows the mothering, nurturing side of women (and sometimes of men)

IV

The

Emperor

ZODIAC SIGN: ARIES
KEY WORDS: AGGRESSION;
STRENGTH

The Emperor card can indicate a man of authority, especially one with greying or white hair. It therefore can represent a boss, father or professional person with administrative powers. Sometimes this card represents an unyielding or severe person who is determined to get what he wants at all costs. Endurance is indicated; a person who has achieved things through great determination is implied. Characteristics of this card are power, stability, or dominance of a situation. Authority and healthy boundaries will play a role in one's life, as will following the rules, playing the game, and receiving the well deserved acknowledgement from the above. Symbolically the Emperor shows the mature, older, more seasoned side of men (and sometimes women).

THE HIEROPHANT

V

The Hierophant

ZODIAC SIGN: TAURUS
KEY WORDS: TRADITIONS;
ESTABLISHED VALUES

This Tarot Trump is the major marriage card. When the Hierophant comes up, a marriage (which is very traditional) is indicated. This card can also indicate conventional religious activities (in a church, synagogue, etc.) or large institutions like the government; large businesses and non-profit corporations can be under the domain of the Hierophant also. Besides marriage, this card can also indicate divorce, especially near the Justice Card #11. It can also indicate a formalized partnership in business, like forming a corporation or the merging of two large companies into a conglomerate. A Hierophant was a priest of ancient Greece who ruled the masses of people, and so the idea of large groups of people, institutions and traditions all go together in this card.

VI

The Lovers

ZODIAC SIGN: GEMINI
KEY WORDS: COMMUNICATION;
CHOICE; LOVE

The Lovers card represents a strong love relationship with good communication and positive growth for both partners. (Compare this card to the Devil #15 which can be the negative side of a relationship.) A karmic relationship (if one believes in Karma) is shown because of the intensity between the two people. Peace and harmony are also indicated, as the picture in the card is reminiscent of the Garden of Eden.

In instances not pertaining to romance, this card will indicate a choice will have to be made. In the older versions of the Lovers card, a man is shown standing between an older and a younger woman—either his mother and his wife or his wife and younger mistress. A cupid is overhead. The meaning is that he has to make a choice.

Next to the Moon card, or 5 or 7 of Swords, a secret love affair is indicated. Near a work card (3 of Pentacles, 8 of Pentacles or in the #6 position of the Horoscope Wheel Spread) a love affair with a co-worker is very possible.

VII

The Chariot

ZODIAC SIGN: CANCER
KEY WORDS: INITIATING;
DETERMINED

he Chariot is a vehicle for travel, and can also indicate great success. This card represents new beginnings, which will be faced with great determination. Triumph and success are shown due to a fixity of purpose. This card can mean an important trip, can indicate long distance travel, or indicate that a person is coming to visit from out of town (usually a male). Independence in thought and deed is portrayed in this card. Near the 9 or 10 of Swords, beware of difficulties in travel. This card near the Sun or 3 of Cups can mean a new car that the querent will be really pleased with. Near difficult cards (3, 9 or 10 of Swords or 5 of Pentacles) this card can indicate car repairs will be needed; near the 5 or 7 of Cups, oil could be leaking in a car. The Chariot next to the Tower can suggest a car accident—the querent should be careful driving during the time frame covered.

One's mind could be exploring new ideas or philosophies—this card requires action—physically, mentally and/or spiritually.

VIII

Strength

ZODIAC SIGN: LEO
KEY WORDS: STRENGTH; PATIENCE

The Strength card indicates courage and an inner strength coming to the surface; however, it also says that patience is needed. Control and endurance are shown; insecurities are not justified. The querent will have the strength to endure in spite of obstacles. This card sometimes indicates getting outdoors, communing with nature or going to a warm climate (notice the warm colors). It also means more vitality, healthwise, and more energy—a very good card in health matters. Inner peace is the reward of this card.

A fondness for animals or the arrival of a new four-legged friend can be another meaning for this card. Near the 4 of Swords an illness or death of a pet can be shown.

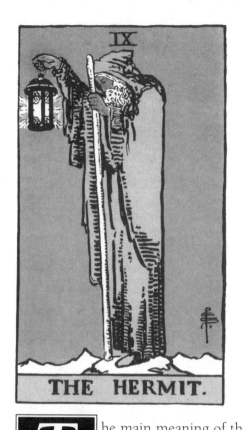

THE HERMIT.

IX

The Hermit

ZODIAC SIGN: VIRGO
KEY WORDS: DISCRIMINATION;
STUDY

The main meaning of the Hermit card is going back to school for formal or informal studies. Many times a great interest in occult matters is indicated, along with meditation or a time of solitude. The Hermit shows the querent analyzing and reevaluating a situation. One who teaches, or conversely, one who is searching for information and alternate meanings, is portrayed. This card suggests a time for withdrawal socially in order to come to terms with oneself. Wisdom and significant insights into a problem are the positive effects of this card, excessive solitude and withdrawal are the negative ones. Sometimes this card means that one becomes more health-conscious—taking vitamins, going on a diet, and becoming more discriminating about one's food intake and body.

The Hermit card can also indicate writing, or keeping a journal of one's thoughts; near the Moon card, a dream journal might be kept.

WHEEL of FORTUNE.

X

Wheel of Fortune

PLANET: JUPITER
KEY WORDS: EXPANSION;
GOOD LUCK

The Wheel of Fortune is the Destiny card. Fate has taken a hand in things. This is a very fortunate card, almost always indicating a change for the better in business and career matters. With this card "even if you try to mess things up, you can't." It indicates being in the right place at the right time. Growth or success in many directions is shown, with or without one's efforts. A kind of divine protection is indicated. This card located near the Lovers or Ace of Cups, will bring a fatefulness to the beginning or continuation of a relationship.

XI

Justice

ZODIAC SIGN: LIBRA
KEY WORDS: BALANCE;
DECISIONS

The Justice card represents legal matters occurring which can be as big as a major lawsuit or as trivial as a parking ticket. Legal matters will be settled in one's favor only if one deserves it. "You reap what you sow." The figure in the card is not blindfolded, therefore Justice is not blind but cosmically impartial. Balance and self-satisfaction through accomplishments are indicated. This card can portray one weighing and balancing a situation, or that a balance will be reached between two forces: work and play, friends and family or freedom and responsibilities, for example. It also can mean signing contracts and/or consulting with a lawyer.

THE HANGED MAN.

XII

The Hanged Man

PLANET: NEPTUNE
KEY WORDS: SACRIFICE,
SPIRITUAL INSIGHTS

The Hanged Man can indicate that sacrifice or martyrdom is happening and it's frequently because of another person. Sometimes the querent may be creating his own self-undoing. Internal struggles are indicated but with great spiritual growth. Efforts and sacrifices will have to be made in order to succeed and/or for a goal to be reached. As the Hanged Man is hanging upside-down, this can indicate a reversal in how one looks at things. The material drives take a back seat to the spiritual ideals. Another meaning for this card can be that the querent is in a state of self-imposed suspended animation, a state of not making decisions or taking action. This is a good card for meditation, yoga, and taking time out for oneself to reflect upon things. Solitude is a good thing to experience with this card.

XIII

Death

ZODIAC SIGN: SCORPIO
KEY WORDS: REGENERATION;
RENEWAL

The Death card indicates the ending of one situation, and the beginning of another. It shows change (dramatically) and rebirth. Compared to the Judgement Card #20, which is a great psychological change, the Death card implies a change of physical circumstances; i.e., new friends, different living conditions or a job change. This card signifies the end of the matter; completion. In regards to health it does NOT mean a physical death, only a change in one's health—sometimes for the better. A more spiritual outlook and less material outlook is indicated. In the card, the king, representing material and worldly success, is lying on the ground and the woman and child are kneeling. But the priest who has faith, is standing. This standing figure (the priest) has a belief system (his spirtual ideals) and so does not fear Death (change).

TEMPERANCE.

XIV

Temperance

ZODIAC SIGN: SAGITTARIUS
KEY WORDS: BLENDING;
BALANCING

The Temperance card indicates that moderation is needed. The Archangel Michael is shown holding two cups in the alchemical process of blending (tempering) and refining two different properties to create a third. The Archangel in the card has one foot in the water and the other on land; water symbolizes the unconscious mind and earth symbolizes the conscious mind. This card signifies getting in touch with one's inner being and the integration of self. It can mean that this is a time to slow down and/or use caution. In some instances it can indicate a problem with alcohol or represent someone who is an alcoholic. In most instances, though, this card shows the querent as finding more peace and harmony in his life, by combining different elements to create the correct formula for personal success.

XV

The Devil

ZODIAC SIGN: CAPRICORN
KEY WORDS: RESTRICTIONS;
MATERIAL ACHIEVEMENTS

I n the Devil card, hard work and restrictions are indicated but often with financial rewards following. This card can indicate a feeling of entrapment in a situation, and not seeing and/or not wanting to change a difficult situation. Since the chains around the two people in the card are not tight, the restrictions can be temporary. A preoccupation with money and material possessions to the exclusion of all else can be indicated. As this is the negative side of the Lovers card, an obsessive partnership or love relationship which is not beneficial to one or both partners can be shown, although the Devil card definitely can indicate good sex! In some cases this card can show a dependency on drugs for personal or medical reasons. When this card shows up in a health question, medication will be started, increased or decreased, depending on the other cards around. Near the Justice card, the Devil can indicate dishonesty in legal matters or connections with the underworld (organized crime). The very basic feelings of this card are obligations and restrictions and/or stubbornness, and being fixed on a potentially destructive course of action, if not moderated.

THE TOWER.

XVI

The Tower

PLANET: MARS
KEY WORDS: ENERGY; UPHEAVAL

Most often the Tower card simply means a change of residence. If you think about it, nothing is as unsettling as having to move, even if it's a positive move. It also can mean remodeling one's home or can indicate that a lot of energy is put into the home. The sudden and unexpected events associated with this card can also imply that someone is moving into or out of the house. Enormous energy is expended in a situation. Also, the Tower can mean electrical repairs in the home or near the Moon, plumbing problems. When the Tower is near the 8 of Wands or the Chariot, a move out of state is possible.

On a different note, the Tower can show flashes of intuition and/or revelations of insight. The lightning hitting the top of the Tower can act like a flashbulb going off in someone's head. Therefore, this can be a very positive card for writers, scientists or others who do mental work. One could be inspired, tested or highly energized.

Healthwise, the Tower can show migraine headaches, or more seriously, a stroke.

THE STAR.

XVII

The Star

ZODIAC SIGN: AQUARIUS
KEY WORDS: COMMUNICATION;
INSPIRATION

T he Star card represents success, recognition, and/or fame. It is the card of anyone who works with the public, from a movie star or an entertainer to a receptionist, waitress, or salesperson. Because the woman in the card has no clothes on, she is obviously visible. Attention grabbing clothing and jewelry may be worn to get the querent noticed, and the limelight will be seeking him, if he is not seeking it. This is the card of the writer, artist, or musician and sometimes it can represent an astrologer. It denotes inspiration and hope. This card can mean a promotion at work or one who deals with computers (which is an Aquarian inspired vocation). A person who communicates well, especially through the written word, is indicated. Also the querent could be in print (newspapers or magazines), or have media coverage (television, radio, or internet). Communication goes well whenever the Star card shows up.

XVIII

The Moon

ZODIAC SIGN: PISCES
KEY WORDS: INTUITION;
DECEPTION

The Moon card indicates that things on the surface are not what they appear to be, and that things which had seemed obvious to you will become less clear; often hidden facts will soon surface. Caution is advised because of unknown factors. Deception and/or jealousy can be indicated. Near the Lovers card, a secret love affair is implied. The Moon card also shows psychic abilities and that the person may experience precognitive dreams that will come true. This is a great time to keep a dream diary. If it appears next to the 7 of Cups, the Moon especially indicates illusions and self-deception. The Moon can indicate an emphasis on the subconscious mind and of listening to one's emotions rather than one's intellect. For men, this card can sometimes mean a strong attachment to their mother, positive or negative, and/or a problem relating to women in general.

This card is connected with fluids and water. In health questions, it can indicate water retention. Near the 3 of Swords, high blood pressure is probable. Since the Moon is hidden and beneath the surface, this card in rare instances can indicate cancer, the disease of cells growing rampant unknown to the person.

This card is also connected to the night and therefore near a work card can mean working at night.

XIX

The Sun

PLANET: SUN
KEY WORDS: EGO; SUCCESS

Simply put, the Sun is the best card in the deck. It therefore can negate or soften most bad cards around it. Happiness, fulfillment of dreams, pleasure in daily living, success and accomplishments are all indicated. The Sun in astrology represents the ego of man, and in the Tarot deck represents the innermost essence of what people strive to attain. If you think about how all life on earth is sustained through the sun—we get our light, heat and energy from it— you can see some of this card's significance. Health will improve and one will radiate energy and happiness. A period of good fortune is near. Things will work out best for all concerned, and the querent should feel good about things, or at the very least much better than he has in a long time.

XX

Judgement

PLANET: PLUTO
KEY WORDS: AWAKENING;
INSIGHT

The Judgement card indicates revival, rejuvenation, and a change in attitude. Things are viewed in a different light and so they become different. A revelation or awakening is indicated as opposed to a change of circumstances as shown by the Death card. Emotional upheaval may be experienced, along with the transformation of ideals or life goals. A person will start doing the very things he thought he would never do. Judgement also shows surprises and one should expect the unexpected; great insights are common with this card. The querent's psychic abilities open, and his inner voice provides unexpected answers if he takes the time to listen to them.

THE WORLD.

XXI
The World

PLANET: SATURN
KEY WORDS: COMPLETION;
EXPANSION

The World card most often indicates an overseas or long-distance trip. It can represent visitors from overseas, dealings with foreigners, and/or imports and exports in business. This is the final goal to which all the other Major Arcana cards have led, therefore completion and fulfillment are indicated. This card shows expansion and the broadening of one's interests, circle of friends and knowledge. Travel to foreign countries and meeting new people are both an excellent way to expand one's awareness. Growth is indicated–through both a broader mental outlook and through new physical or psychic experiences.

I would like to explain why Saturn is associated with the World card. In astrology Saturn is often the taskmaster that causes one to work hard and can bring limitations. But on the plus side, Saturn brings rewards for that hard work to those who have earned it . The World card signifies those rewards.

The

Minor

Arcana

The Minor Arcana

There are 56 Minor Arcana cards. These cards relate in more detail to specific events in a person's life; they represent the people and events that apply more to everyday living. The four Aces of the Minor Arcana all show new beginnings and new opportunities. (See the numerology for the number 1.) The sixteen "court" cards (Pages, Knights, Queens and Kings) will usually represent the people in the querent's life.

Court cards are so named because the King, Queen, Knight and Page were the people who made up the court in past times. Court cards will indicate people 99% of the time. The other 1% of the time the Pages will indicate the <u>start</u> of a new event coming into the querent's life, Knights will indicate the <u>action</u> of an event, Queens the <u>stability</u> of an event and Kings the <u>completion</u> of an event. Many times the Page, Knight and King of the same suit are interchangeable; a Page and King in the same spread and of the same suit may be the same person. (Or the Knight and King, etc. may be the same person.)

The four suits are divided as follows:

WANDS:
Wands are associated with change, inspiration, and enterprise. They represent the element of fire and the summer season, when leaves grow on the trees.

SWORDS:
Swords are associated with intellect, conflict and challenges. They represent the air element and the winter season, when life was hard and most people struggled.

CUPS:
Cups are associated with love, emotions and spiritual ideals. They represent the element of water and the autumn season, when marriages most often took place in medieval times.

PENTACLES:
Pentacles are associated with money, material goods, and personal values. They represent the earth element and the spring season, when commerce would begin again and trades would flourish.

ACE of WANDS.

Ace
Of
Wands

In the Ace of Wands card, a hand emerges from a cloud, and holds a living, growing tree branch or wand.

This card indicates a new opportunity will soon be presented to the querent. Also, this card many times will represent a trip and contact with out of town people, bringing new ideas through new people and places. It's a great time to expand your horizons through travel. A letter, phone call or E-mail can bring information of new opportunities. The Ace of Wands indicates an action-oriented undertaking or enterprise. An opportunity will be presented, but it is up to the individual to act upon it.

II
Of
Wands

 n the 2 of Wands card, a person who has control of his life or control of a situation is shown, as depicted by the man holding the world in his hand.

An influential person or man of property may affect one's life. If the querent doesn't give his power to another, then he will be taking control of his life and looking at aspects of it where *he* is the authority. Success and long term planning are indicated as the querent is looking at the big picture and settling into a plan of action. Sometimes this card may indicate dealings with property, such as buying, selling or remodeling a home. The 2 of Wands sometimes represents a house with a terrace or patio. Next to the Devil, this card can mean major repairs around the home; next to the Moon this card can be major plumbing repairs.

III
Of
Wands

 n the 3 of Wands card, a man stands on a hilltop, his back to us, overlooking a yellow sea.

This card can mean turning one's back on a situation, as shown by the man's back in the card, and/or is the man in the card looking to the future for better things? In cases where there are two or more different meanings for the card, you must look at the surrounding cards to decide which definition applies and follow your instincts. A decision may be reached and firmly adhered to, and often one will be looking at a problem with detachment and with a more grounded approach.

This card can also indicate dealings with property or decisions around the home. Stability in the home is indicated, as are long term investments and improvements.

One's back is turned on past events as the querent looks calmly toward future endeavors.

IV

Of

Wands

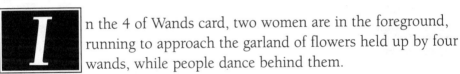

In the 4 of Wands card, two women are in the foreground, running to approach the garland of flowers held up by four wands, while people dance behind them.

This card can mean going to a celebration or party. It denotes good news, especially unexpected *welcomed* visitors, and children around the house. When it comes up, this card means getting out of one's house more and socializing more. New friends, happiness, joy and fun with friends are all indicated. Relax and let things come to you, this card is saying.

V
Of
Wands

In the 5 of Wands card, five men are at odds with one another, wielding wands as if in battle.

This card indicates arguments and conflicts. The 5 of Wands can also express an internal struggle, with the querent at war with himself. Sometimes competition is a meaning for this card. Emotional stress, or nervous disorders are also prominent. It is the only Wands card in which the wands are pointed in different directions, showing disharmony and turmoil around the person. Remember that different viewpoints can open one up to different ways of looking at things. Healthwise, this card can indicate stomach problems or the beginning of an ulcer.

VI
Of
Wands

 n the 6 of Wands card, a man is seated upon a horse, with people walking along side. He has a laurel wreath both on his head and on the wand he holds.

Victory is shown, as the laurel wreath was a symbol of victory and held sacred to Apollo, the Sun God. The two laurel wreaths indicate success in an undertaking. The 6 of Wands card can also mean a visitor coming in from out of town, or that the querent will be taking a journey. (Whenever there are horses in the cards, travel can be indicated.) Occasionally this card can indicate leadership abilities and denote one who is capable of leading a group or groups of people.

VII
Of
Wands

In the 7 of Wands card, a man is standing on top of a hill with a wand, holding off six other wands.

This card shows a person who anticipates a struggle. Caution is needed–there may be many obstacles. The obstacles, however, may be imaginary, as the picture in the card does not show those who are holding the wands. This card can mean success through endurance and also feeling pressured or defensive. The querent may be on top of things, but his position needs to be guarded to be maintained, and he should stay vigilant. Tension is indicated.

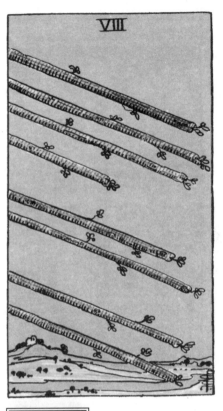

VIII

Of

Wands

In the 8 of Wands card, eight wands fly through the air aimed toward a destination.

Most often the meaning of this card is a trip; especially by plane. It can also indicate acting upon something hastily (as shown by the movement of the wands), or the resolution of a problem (the wands are nearing their destination). This card also can indicate speed, suddenness, swift activity and/or sudden progress. Just as the wands near their destination in the card, the querent is approaching a much needed (fill in the blank) rest, vacation or resolution of a problem.

IX

Of

Wands

In the 9 of Wands card, a man with a bandaged head leans on a wand, while eight wands are aligned behind him.

This card indicates a person who is backed into a corner. He is battle-scarred (as indicated by his bandaged head) but is prepared to face challenges. The wands in the row behind him serve as a back-up or for defense. It's time to pause and re-assess the situation. Even if excessive pressures or problems are happening, this card shows that the querent may be feeling too defensive about something. Caution is needed but fear is not. The 7 and 9 of Wands together mean one should slow down and be more thoughtful and thorough with decisions, while staying detached from the pressures.

X
Of
Wands

In the 10 of Wands card, a man carrying ten wands heads toward a village.

This card indicates that a burden will soon be lifted, as shown by the man walking toward the village to deliver his wands. Troubles will soon be resolved. The light is at the end of the tunnel and the project the querent has been putting his energy into nears completion. This card can mean striving either to meet a goal or to maintain a certain level or position. A lot of problems around the querent will soon be alleviated, even if presently there are heavy responsibilities.

The tens of the four suits represent endings (completions) of cycles.

PAGE of WANDS.

Page Of Wands

ELEMENT: FIRE

The Page of Wands represents a light, blond haired, blue-eyed person. If representing a child, the Page can be male or female. If representing a youth (teenager), the Page will usually be a male.

KNIGHT of WANDS.

Knight
Of
Wands

ZODIAC SIGN ASSOCIATED:
SAGITTARIUS

he Knight of Wands represents an adult man, blue-eyed with light or greying hair, usually from out of town or one who travels with his work. He may be a salesman.

Often Knights are unmarried men from out of town or those who travel with their work.

Queen Of Wands

ZODIAC SIGN ASSOCIATED: LEO

The Queen of Wands is a fair haired (blond)* woman with blue eyes. This card can represent a career-oriented woman. She may be sympathetic and understanding. Queens, being women, have no age limitations. They can be from their early twenties upward.

*Is the haircoloring natural or from a bottle? *Usually* this will represent the color the woman has at the time of the reading.

King Of Wands

ZODIAC SIGN ASSOCIATED: ARIES

he King of Wands is a mature blond or grey haired man with blue eyes. He is usually married, and agewise in his mid 30's and upwards. He is an honest and conscientious person, many times a sharp business man, who is good with people.

Ace
Of
Cups

In the Ace of Cups card, an open hand holds a cup with a dove overhead, while water flows both upwards and downwards.

The Ace of Cups traditionally represents a new love and the indication of a very important love relationship coming. For someone already in a committed relationship, the opportunity is still there even though the person may not act upon it. It can also indicate a new love of a hobby or interest that gets one's creative juices flowing. There could be an addition to the family–a child, grandchild, puppy or kitten (computer or television)– anything that will bring long term pleasure.

II
Of
Cups

In the 2 of Cups card, a lion's head with wings hovers above the man and woman toasting each other.

The 2 of Cups can represent an engagement or commitment in a love relationship. Or, it also can mean less intensely, a friendship or business partnership. Harmony and good communication between two people are shown here, along with cooperation and unity. The querent will become more considerate of the other person in his life and compromises will be reached on issues that have been bothersome.

III
Of
Cups

In the 3 of Cups card, there are 3 women raising their cups in a joyous dance.

This card represents a happy occasion. Celebrating is common and parties are indicated (especially with liquor). Close, sister-like friends may be in your environment. Other women are being supportive. Conclusion or fulfillment of a situation is indicated. More physical activity is possible, and a dance class or aerobics class could be on the horizon. On the negative side, the querent or someone around him could be using liquor in excess, and waking up with a hangover or two.

IV
Of
Cups

n the 4 of Cups card, a person is sitting by a tree, gazing at three cups while another cup, held by a hand, is suspended in mid-air.

There are two very different ways of interpreting this card.

The first is that the person is being offered something he will refuse; it may be, for example, a marriage proposal, a new job, etc. The second meaning is that there will be something unexpected offered to the person, almost as if out of the blue. A new opportunity will be presented that the person is not now aware of. (Does the seated figure see the cup being offered?)

It is up to the reader to look at the other cards in the spread and decide which definition applies. This can also be a card of contemplation, but not a card of decision-making. It indicates one should not act until the answer is crystal clear and the action is thoroughly thought through.

V
Of
Cups

n the 5 of Cups card, a person dressed in a black cloak is looking at the three spilled cups, while ignoring the two cups standing.

A disappointment or partial loss is suggested. As all the cups are not spilled, only a partial regret is felt. The person, however, may focus his energies on the disappointment (spilled cups) and feel guilt, self-incrimination and sadness, while ignoring the standing cups behind him. One may contemplate ending a relationship or friendship, but there may still be some positive feelings here—beware of acting hastily. It's best to feel the sadness, and then let it go. A positive mental attitude will help immensely.

Healthwise, this card can indicate menstrual problems for women, and next to the 10 of Swords, possibly a hysterectomy. This card may simply be fluid problems for men or women, and/or swollen joints.

VI
Of
Cups

In the 6 of Cups card, there are two children talking in a village setting with six cups around them.

In a reading this card means people from the past will be coming back into one's life. Family or children can be prominent or play an important role in the querent's life. The person may be influenced by the past, or dwells in the past. Nostalgia is felt and a longing for childhood security is experienced. Near the 10 of Cups, a happy reunion (family, friends or school) is indicated. If the querent is doing dream work or seeing a therapist, a lot of progress will be made.

VII
Of
Cups

In the 7 of Cups card, a man is looking up at seven cups; each one is filled with a different thought or desire (are they the seven deadly sins?).

This is the card of illusions, delusions and confusion. It can also suggest many choices or opportunities will be offered. Sometimes this card can mean visualizing many things and ideas, or you may be scattering your energy and doing too many things at once. Like the card itself, there are many ways to interpret its meanings. It's best to stay focused on the tried and true while keeping an open mind to new options.

When the 7 of Cups is near a card of property like the 2 of Wands, 3 of Wands or the 9 of Wands, plumbing problems may occur.

Also, circulation problems or high blood pressure can be a health issue with this card, along with water retention. Alcoholism can be a concern.

VIII
Of
Cups

In the 8 of Cups card, a person is walking away from the stacked cups, having already crossed a river.

This card can mean one is ending a relationship, leaving a job or abandoning previous plans. The feeling of turning one's back on a situation or leaving an area of one's life to go on to something else, is foremost in the meaning of this card. Distancing oneself from a person or problem is quite helpful now.

In regards to health, this is a good card for losing weight, as the person may be cutting down on his food intake; he may also be omitting one particular item such as salt or sugar from his diet.

IX
Of
Cups

In the 9 of Cups card, a man is seated in front of a table with nine cups on it, and has a contented look on his face.

This is a card of satisfaction. The person is feeling secure, both emotionally and physically. Success and material attainment are indicated. Although this is quite a happy card (some authors on the Tarot say you will get your wish when this card comes up), the negative side would imply over-indulgence and difficulty in denying oneself anything. Usually, however, a feeling of well being is experienced, along with contentment and the feeling of a job well done.

X
Of
Cups

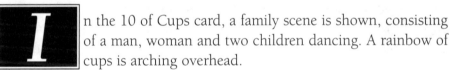

I n the 10 of Cups card, a family scene is shown, consisting of a man, woman and two children dancing. A rainbow of cups is arching overhead.

The picture is almost self-explanatory, indicating contentment and great happiness. This card sometimes indicates a wedding, and is one of three cards in the deck that can indicate a forthcoming marriage. Often it will show a family gathering, reunion or party with children prominent. A happy home and pleasant emotions, such as joy, appreciation, relaxation and love go with this card.

PAGE of CUPS.

Page Of Cups

ELEMENT: WATER

The Page of Cups implies a light brown haired, blue or hazel-eyed person, either male or female if children. The Page could be a young man (through early twenties) with those physical characteristics.

Knight
Of
Cups

ZODIAC SIGN ASSOCIATED: PISCES

he Knight of Cups is a light brown haired, blue or hazel-eyed man, usually unmarried. He can be emotional (being of the suit of Cups) and supportive.

Queen

Of

Cups

ZODIAC SIGN ASSOCIATED:
CANCER

The Queen of Cups represents a light brown haired, blue or hazel-eyed woman. Because she is a Cup, she may be a homebody or housewife. She may also be an artistic woman.

King Of Cups

ZODIAC SIGN ASSOCIATED:
SCORPIO

he King of Cups is a light brown haired, blue or hazel-eyed mature man. Because he is a king, he may be married. He can be artistic and/or religious, and usually is a man mid-30's and older.

Ace Of Swords

ELEMENT: AIR

I n the Ace of Swords card, a hand holding a sword appears out of the sky.

The Ace of Swords indicates triumph, victory and great strength. This is the card of a job change, new job or total career change. Often with this card a person will go into his own business or change to a challenging and unusual business. The Ace of Swords is very fortunate for work when it appears next to the Wheel of Fortune or the Sun card. It is a card of great determination and mental clarity.

II Of Swords

In the 2 of Swords card, a woman is blindfolded, holding two swords crossed over her heart with her back to the sea.

This is the card of a true and loyal friend, one who is "blind" to your faults (she's blindfolded), many times a dark haired woman. This card can also indicate balance and harmony, or status quo. As the woman in the card is sitting quietly with calm waters behind her, this card can also mean patience is needed. You may be waiting for something for a while when this card comes up. It is a very passive card with no action indicated. By staying centered and letting events flow naturally, the querent will be more in tune with his inner feelings and intuition.

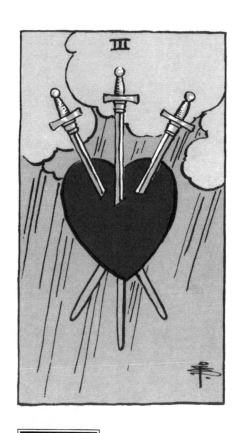

III Of Swords

I n the 3 of Swords card, a heart with three swords in it is shown in front of a background of clouds and falling rain.

This is one of those cards people point to and exclaim, "What does that mean?" Well, it can mean disappointment or heartache. However, this card can very simply mean a delay, separation or postponement, time or spacewise (the swords divide or separate the heart in 3 sections). Many times a person will be separated from a loved one because of a trip or move. Distance and detachment are an asset when this card comes up.

In regards to health, this card indicates heart problems, high blood pressure, poor circulation and/or heart attacks. Unless otherwise strongly indicated, the health problems are not fatal. If next to a court card, that person may experience the health problems, rather than the querent.

IV Of Swords

I n the 4 of Swords card, there is a picture of a person lying on a tomb within a church (look at the stained glass window).

This card can indicate waiting, patience and rest are needed. It sometimes indicates colds or the flu, and feeling tired physically and/or mentally. Emotional depression is suggested and is one of the main meanings of this card. It can indicate a good time for meditating–a good time to absorb knowledge through contemplation. On the negative side, this is the one card that can show a physical death, especially next to the 8, 9 or 10 of Swords or the Judgement card.

I'd like to digress here and talk a little about death in the cards. First of all, death is a very difficult thing to predict.* Since there is great responsibility in reading the cards, you, the reader, must always weigh the possible meanings of each card and select the most appropriate definition. A healthy person getting the 4 of Swords is not going to drop dead that afternoon. He may be depressed, however. Remember, even if the person receiving the reading is skeptical, or tells you that he wants to hear everything, good or bad, the words that you speak will leave an impression on the person. Therefore, I always stress the positive while pointing out what the querent should be prepared for and cautious about.

*I've seen people die just after getting wonderful cards (the Sun, Wheel of Fortune, 10 of Cups, etc.) when they've been terminally ill and death has been a welcomed release for them.

V Of
Swords

 n the 5 of Swords card, a man is holding three swords as he looks at two people who are walking away (in defeat?) with their swords on the ground.

This is a card of deception, so the querent should be aware that things are not as they seem. Caution is advised and one shouldn't take things at face value. There are events transpiring behind the scenes that are not yet known. In a work situation, it can mean changes in management are happening that will be affecting the querent and may come out in the open at a later date. In a love relationship, it can mean someone is watching the querent that he is not consciously aware of, who has not gotten up the nerve to approach him. Next to a court card, this card can mean that that person is not being completely honest with you. A victory can be achieved, but not without a struggle.

VI Of Swords

I n the 6 of Swords card, a man in a boat is ferrying a woman and child across the water.

This card can mean a trip near water. Many times it indicates trips to Michigan or Wisconsin, as these states are not only near water but are usually trips for relaxation and vacationing; also Florida is a frequent destination with this card. Because I live in Chicago, this card can also indicate to me the downtown area which is near Lake Michigan. If it were to come up in a reading about work, then it could mean a job downtown. This is an example of how to personalize the cards for yourself. Occasionally the 6 of Swords literally suggests being on a boat or taking a cruise.

If this card doesn't mean a trip, it can mean leaving troubled waters (the wavy lines) and going into calmer waters (the smooth water) in the card.

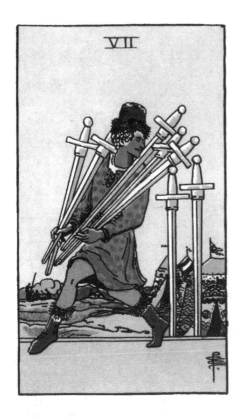

VII Of Swords

 n the 7 of Swords card, a man is sneaking away with five swords while looking over his shoulder at the two swords behind him.

Compare the 5 and 7 of Swords cards. In the 5 of Swords card, someone is deceiving the querent, while in the 7 of Swords card, the querent is deceiving someone else. This may only mean that he is keeping his thoughts to himself, or, in a work situation, it could mean he is making changes (like sending out resumés) and not telling anyone. This card indicates someone who uses secrecy or deception to get what is wanted. One may make plans, but be unsure as to how they'll work–it's a good time to double check all the facts and figures. Since the man in the card is looking over his shoulder to see what is behind him, this card can also mean that the querent is discreetly analyzing his actions and may be cutting his losses and leaving a situation while it's possible to do so.

VIII Of Swords

 n the 8 of Swords card, a woman tied in ropes is surrounded by eight swords; the swords do not completely encircle her, nor are the ropes tight.

When this card comes up you are feeling trapped in a situation, whether in reality you are or not. There are restrictions through a person or an idea, and responsibilities weigh heavy. The querent has to remember that the reflective period this card brings can be most liberating–the looking inward unites the conscious and subconscious mind.

Healthwise, this is a good card to lose weight with, or to go on a restricted diet. It can also mean having tests done in a hospital or an overnight stay in one. Near the legal card (Justice) this could mean having legal restrictions on you. Most times, whatever these restrictions are, they are self-imposed and can be changed through one's own efforts.

IX Of
Swords

n the 9 of Swords card, a person is sitting up and crying in bed while nine swords hang overhead in the black background.

This card implies anxiety, worry and anguish, with the mind working overtime. Often the person is not sleeping well when this card comes up or may be experiencing bad dreams and nightmares due to stress. Also the querent may be blowing things out of proportion, especially when this card is next to the 7 of Cups. It can also mean feeling despair (notice the totally black background). Positive affirmations and emotional detachment to an outcome or person are two helpful ways of working with this card. In regards to health, this card may indicate minor surgery or stomach related problems (brought about through worry), and sometimes ulcers. It can indicate a miscarriage, if other cards collaborate.

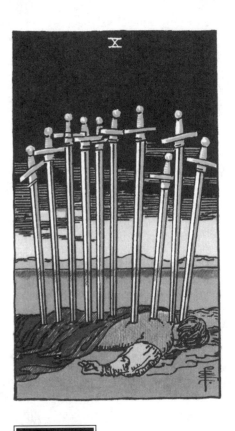

X Of
Swords

In the 10 of Swords card, a man is lying on the ground with ten swords in his back.

This card represents the end of the matter. A turning point is reached, a great catharsis occurs. The querent has reached the bottom and so will now start to move upward. The sky lightening shows new hope. The Swords are in the Chakra (energy) points of the body, and so this card can indicate a spiritual awakening. Pertaining to health, this is the card of major surgery and literally back problems. One needs to be careful of pulled muscles. May times alternative health methods such as acupuncture, massage and holistic remedies can be useful.

PAGE of SWORDS.

Page Of Swords

ELEMENT: AIR

The Page of Swords is a young person, male or female with medium brown hair and brown or hazel eyes. The Page could also be a young man up to his early twenties with those physical characteristics.

The Sword people (court cards of this suit) are generally skilled with their hands and/or are good at working with mechanical things.

KNIGHT of SWORDS .

Knight Of Swords

ZODIAC SIGN ASSOCIATED: GEMINI

he Knight of Swords is a man with medium brown hair and brown or hazel eyes. He usually is a fairly aggressive man and one who is unmarried.

Queen Of Swords

ZODIAC SIGN ASSOCIATED:
AQUARIUS

he Queen of Swords is a woman with medium brown or reddish brown hair and brown or hazel eyes. She is many times an assertive or strong-willed woman.

King Of Swords

ZODIAC SIGN ASSOCIATED:
LIBRA

 The King of Swords is a mature, medium brown haired man with brown or hazel eyes. Being a king, he can be a married man.

Ace
Of
Pentacles

ELEMENT: EARTH

In the Ace of Pentacles card, a hand holding a pentacle comes out of a cloud above a lush garden.

This card indicates an increase in money. Perhaps a raise at work, a refund that's unexpected, or a freelance job appears out of the blue. When it appears next to the Wheel of Fortune or 8 of Pentacles, it indicates a raise at work. Another meaning for this card is a gift, especially a diamond ring or piece of jewelry. When it appears next to the 8 of Wands, or in the 3rd or 9th houses of the horoscope spread, this card can suggest that a check is coming to you in the mail. Basically an opportunity is coming to make more money, when this card appears, and small indulgences for oneself are most appreciated. The querent should remember that an increase in money begins with valuing oneself more.

II
Of
Pentacles

In the 2 of Pentacles card, a man is juggling two pentacles while a rocky sea appears in the background.

This is a card of balance. It can mean balancing money; more money will be coming in, but you will spend it as fast as you make it. Or you may be weighing and balancing an idea, looking at two sides of the coin, so to speak. Indecision comes with this card, and moderation in daily routines is helpful. Three meals a day and eight hours of sleep a night can alleviate some stress. In regards to health, there can be a weight gain followed by a weight loss, or vice versa. One of the concepts for this card is instability. One must weigh all facets of a situation before making a decision, and not rush to a conclusion.

III

Of

Pentacles

I n the 3 of Pentacles card, a craftsman and two religious figures are discussing blueprints in a church.

    This is the card of the craftsman, or one skilled with his
hands. Artistic abilities are also indicated and the querent's artistic and
creative side may become more prominent. A new skill is learned or mas-
tered. Since the setting of the card is in a church, this sometimes can suggest a marriage or that the querent will be attending a wedding. This is
also the card of groups or organizations. The querent may be attending a
social function sponsored by a group or organization; business meetings
also may be prominent.

IV
Of
Pentacles

 n the 4 of Pentacles card, a man is seated in front of a city with a pentacle on his head and two beneath his feet, while he firmly grasps a fourth one.

The querent will be able to save more money than he has been able to do in the past. This is the card of holding on to things. If the reading pertains to a relationship, the person is holding on to the relationship and is unwilling to let go of it. The 4 of Pentacles indicates a good time to stock up on things, but not necessarily to gamble or speculate or take risks. This card can also indicate a person who carries possessiveness to an extreme and is a hoarder or pack rat. Besides holding onto material possessions, the 4 of Pentacles indicates that in other areas of life, the querent may be inflexible with new ideas or new ways of doing things.

V
Of
Pentacles

n the 5 of Pentacles card, two forlorn people are walking past a church in the snow. One of them is on crutches, both are in rags.

The querent will be spending more money than anticipated, perhaps on a major purchase (car, home, etc.) Therefore this card indicates worry about money. It can suggest a money loss, and is a very bad card if it comes up in matters of speculation. Near the Moon or 7 of Swords, one should use caution in regards to valuables to prevent loss or theft. In travelling, be aware of your possessions so that nothing is stolen and that your luggage gets on the right flight–traveller's checks would be a good idea.

A very different meaning for this card is insecurity; the person doesn't feel good about himself and has feelings of low self-esteem. His sense of lack extends into his personal life, so positive thinking and affirmations can be very helpful. The people in the card are passing a church looking down, indicating that they are ignoring their belief system or possibly need to renew their faith and/or find other spiritual guidance.

VI
Of
Pentacles

I n the 6 of Pentacles card, a merchant is handing coins to two beggars.

This is the card of unexpected money, often money that is not earned. This card can represent winning some money, getting a grant or scholarship, or possibly collecting on an insurance policy or lawsuit. This card can also represent an income tax refund. People who work on commission often get this card, indicating a lump sum of money. It can be a retroactive pay increase. And sometimes this card can represent a loan coming through or a small inheritance. Almost always extra money comes with this card, and the querent should relax and indulge himself a bit.

VII
Of
Pentacles

In the 7 of Pentacles card, a man is resting on his hoe, gazing at vines which have pentacles growing on them.

This card indicates growth and analyzing that growth. The man in the card is looking at the pentacles growing on the bush and thinking about them. It's the time to look at what you've created, put your priorities in order, and make plans for the next step. This card may show that money is not bringing you satisfaction (or that a job, love relationship, etc. is not bringing it). The man in the card is wearing one brown shoe and one orange shoe. The color brown represents practicality, the color orange ambition. Another meaning for this card is success through hard work and ambition.

VIII
Of
Pentacles

In the 8 of Pentacles card, a man is seated at a workbench chiseling pentacles onto circular disks.

This card often means that a person will be working long or longer hours, or holding down two jobs. It is also the card of skill and talent and as such, can show that a person has a skill for needlepoint, sewing, cooking, woodworking, etc. (things that require manual dexterity).

The 8 of Pentacles can indicate work or analysis is needed in a relationship if it is next to the Lovers or in handling money if it is next to the 2 of Pentacles. It indicates that by diligent work, success is attained.

IX
Of
Pentacles

I n the 9 of Pentacles card, a woman stands in a garden of pentacles while a falcon rests on her hand.

This card symbolizes material well-being which includes comfort, security and stability. It can have to do with buying or selling property, or dealings with a woman who owns property and money. This is a card representing accomplishments and enjoying the fruits of one's labors. Projects you've worked on and investments you've made are paying off.

The 9 of Pentacles also can indicate people who garden or love to have plants around them. Activities concerning the Earth are satisfying now–from gardening to hiking to joining an environmentally conscious organization.

X
Of
Pentacles

 n the 10 of Pentacles card, a grey haired man is seated near a man, woman and child. The pentacles are arranged in the form of the Tree of Life of the Kaballah.

The 10 of Pentacles is the big money card; a large amount of money is forthcoming. Sometimes the money comes from an insurance settlement, an inheritance, an income tax refund, or speculation. If the card appears in the fifth position of the Astrology Wheel Spread, this would especially indicate winning some money. My formula for winning the lottery is the Wheel of Fortune next to the 10 of Pentacles.

Besides getting money, this card symbolizes success and recognition (especially next to the Star). Sometimes it indicates guidance from an older person who would hold or invest one's money, and family is sometimes involved.

Page
Of
Pentacles

ELEMENT: EARTH

he Page of Pentacles represents a dark haired, brown-eyed person, either male or female if a child, or a young man through his early twenties. He is practical and work oriented.

KNIGHT of PENTACLES.

Knight Of Pentacles

ZODIAC SIGN ASSOCIATED: VIRGO

 he Knight of Pentacles suggests a man with dark brown hair and brown eyes, usually unmarried. Agewise, he is from his mid-twenties upward.

Queen Of Pentacles

ZODIAC SIGN ASSOCIATED: CAPRICORN

The Queen of Pentacles characteristically is a dark brown haired woman with brown eyes. The Queen of Pentacles has a sadness that can indicate she is a divorced or widowed woman.

King

Of

Pentacles

ZODIAC SIGN ASSOCIATED:
TAURUS

he King of Pentacles represents a man with dark brown hair and brown eyes. Usually the King of Pentacles has his own business or works for himself. He can be a married man.

Spread

and

Comments

The Spreads

In doing a reading, it is very important to make yourself comfortable and to feel relaxed. If you are uneasy or apprehensive for any reason while reading for someone, you will not have as good results as you might have otherwise. I don't read reversed cards—I always put them right side up. It makes the ideas and images flow easier for me. In looking at a spread, the cards should "talk" to you. Think of them as nouns or verbs that you are putting together to create a sentence or paragraph. You should have a basic meaning of every card in your mind, but also look at the overall meaning of the cards together. Sometimes one particular card will stand out to you—that one card can give you the definite answer to the question or contain the most important message for the querent.

The person shuffling the cards should be made to feel at ease. I tell my clients to shuffle until they feel comfortable (which can take some people quite a long time) and then to cut once with his/her left hand. I use the left hand to cut the cards because it is the hand closest to the heart. Next, the cards that were on the bottom of the deck are put on the top.

THE CELTIC CROSS SPREAD

This spread is used to answer a specific question— not for a general reading. I have the querent think about his question while shuffling the deck.

After shuffling and cutting the deck as described above, you lay the cards out as numbered. The significator is the card that *signifies* the person who the question is about. Whatever card comes up for #1A will tell you the person's feelings about the question. Although the meanings for the positions of the cards are given, it is important to get the overall view of the cards and notice if the colors are particularly bright or dark. And remember that not every card may make sense to you. Sometimes a court card shows up and you don't know who it represents. Well, it may represent someone the querent is yet to meet. Or a card may represent an event which makes no sense to you. Don't let this be an obstacle to reading the cards. You will still get information that is useful. The second row of cards goes more into the future in general.

Remember, you can adjust the timing of the spread. If a person asks if he will get a job next week, then card #10 would be next week, card #3 would be 3-4 days from now and card #6 would be tomorrow, timewise.

THE ASTROLOGY WHEEL SPREAD

This spread is used as a general, three-month forecast; things that come up will happen in the 3-month time period, although you won't know *exactly* when, except for card #1A.

Whatever appears in position #1A will probably happen within 1 month or be happening right now.

The card in the #1 position represents the person. If a King or Knight shows up and you are reading for a woman, it does not mean the woman will have a sex change operation, (although that could be a possibility). Probably the woman will be seen as more assertive or aggressive. The 8 of Cups or 8 of Swords would indicate a weight change, in position #1. A court card of a different hair coloring can indicate the querent lightening or darkening his hair, in position #1.

The Devil card in the 8th house can mean a problem with taxes, especially around tax time (Feb.-May). I have seen it mean an audit from the IRS. But of course, it can mean other things (feeling restricted, an intense relationship, etc.) also.

I usually look at cards 2, 6 and 10 together to see money and work in general.

THE HEALTH SPREAD

This spread is used to analyze a person's present health condition.

After the cards are laid out (in the shape of the body) you read it this way: If a 'negative' card shows up in a given spot, that is where the person is experiencing health problems. The back is indicated by cards #1, #3 (shoulders) and #4.

The 3 of Swords in the #1 position (chest) is especially indicative of heart problems. The 9 of Cups in the #7 position (stomach) can show a weight gain; the 8 of Cups there, a weight loss. The #2 position (head) sometimes shows a person's attitude toward life. Mostly it would be physical, though. For example, I once read a woman who got the Tower card in the #2 position and she got migraine headaches!

Movement cards by the feet (#10 and #11), i.e., Knights or the Chariot or the 6 or 8 of Wands, could indicate the person will start exercising (jogging or dancing). Court cards are neutral, and the rule of things is to just look for cards of adversity. The Moon card, or 5 or 7 of Swords, can indicate hidden problems. Sometimes the Moon is water retention. The Moon can also represent cancer, but I would be cautious in making that diagnosis.

Again, patterns can and should be adapted to the particular needs and intuitions of the reader and/or client.

THE TREE OF LIFE SPREAD

In this layout, only the Major Arcana are used. This is not used as a predictive spread, but rather as a personality evaluation. The querent shuffles and cuts the 22 cards. They are laid out as indicated.

I have seen the Devil card come up in the #1 position (the person's highest ideals) which did not mean the person was evil, but probably either very materialistic or very fixed in his point of view. The Hermit in the #5 position can mean the querent is very self-critical or over-analyzes things to a fault. And so you take the basic meanings of the card and fit them into each placement.

THE PYRAMID SPREAD

This spread is used as a general one year forecast. In most cases the first card up is the next month, unless you are doing the reading in the first week of that month. Then it would be the month you're in now.

If a Court card comes up in position #1, that person will be prominent for the querent that month. (You don't know how, so use your intuition.)

Many times when the difficult cards are next to a Court card, the person represented by the Court card will be having the problems, not the person you are reading for.

If the last card (28) of the pyramid is either unclear or indicates problems, I lay out one or two more cards to clarify the meaning.

This spread is great for seeing an overview for the year coming up. You can, for example, see what month a person will be changing jobs or moving. Sometimes it's easy to get caught up in the cards and forget to give the month that the event is happening, but that's what makes this spread so valuable. So please try to remember to incorporate the time frame while doing the reading.

THE 3 MONTH SPREAD

This is a general reading for the next 3 months. The cards are read independently of each other, with each card showing an event for that week.

This is a good spread to reinforce the Celtic Cross or Astrology Wheel Spread and perhaps get a more accurate time frame. You can expand this idea and do a weekly spread of 7 cards, right to left to get even more specific.

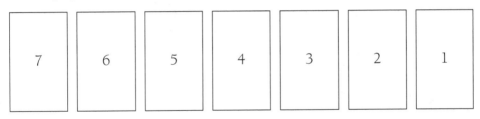

A word to the wise—don't get carried away with the daily, weekly or monthly readings! They can become too much of a good thing which then becomes a mass of confusion. ("Discretion is the better part of valor," to throw in an old cliché.)

The Celtic Cross

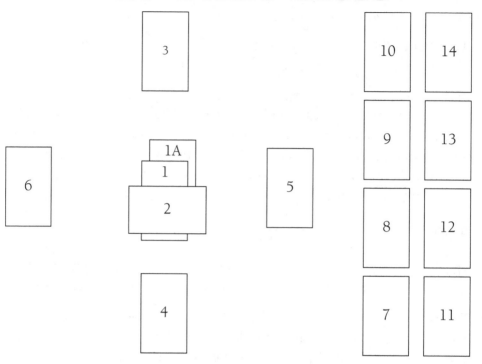

1A. The Significicator
  1. The Immediate Situation (within 1 month's time)
  2. Obstacles (if a good card, then possibly a delay for that card)
  3. Distant Future (within 6 month's time)
  4. Near Past   ⎫
  5. Distant Past   ⎬ (I look at 4 and 5 together as past events)
                     ⎭
  6. Near Future (within 3 month's time)
  7. More About The Person
  8. The Environment of the Question
  9. Person's Hopes or Fears
10. The Outcome
If a court card is in position #10, that means that a person (represented by the court card) will have a great influence in the outcome.
11. The 2nd Year (beginning of)
12. The 2nd Year (middle of)
13. The 2nd Year (later part of)
14. The 2nd Year (end of)

Occasionally a 3rd row of cards can be helpful to look further into time, 3 years from now. I don't recommend doing more than 3 rows, as many things can change.

The Astrology Spread
3 Month General

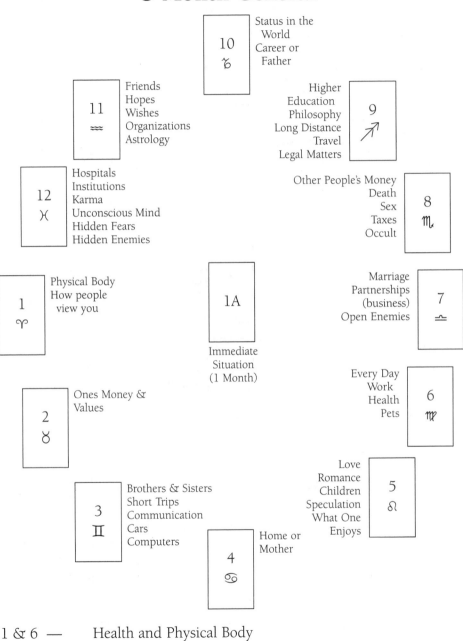

10 ♑ — Status in the World, Career or Father

11 ♒ — Friends, Hopes, Wishes, Organizations, Astrology

9 ♐ — Higher Education, Philosophy, Long Distance Travel, Legal Matters

12 ♓ — Hospitals, Institutions, Karma, Unconscious Mind, Hidden Fears, Hidden Enemies

8 ♏ — Other People's Money, Death, Sex, Taxes, Occult

1 ♈ — Physical Body, How people view you

1A — Immediate Situation (1 Month)

7 ♎ — Marriage, Partnerships (business), Open Enemies

2 ♉ — Ones Money & Values

6 ♍ — Every Day, Work, Health, Pets

3 ♊ — Brothers & Sisters, Short Trips, Communication, Cars, Computers

4 ♋ — Home or Mother

5 ♌ — Love, Romance, Children, Speculation, What One Enjoys

1 & 6 —	Health and Physical Body
2-6-10 —	Work
4-8-12 —	Psychic Events
1-7 —	Person and his/her partner
3-9 —	Travel (short distances and long distances)

The Health Spread

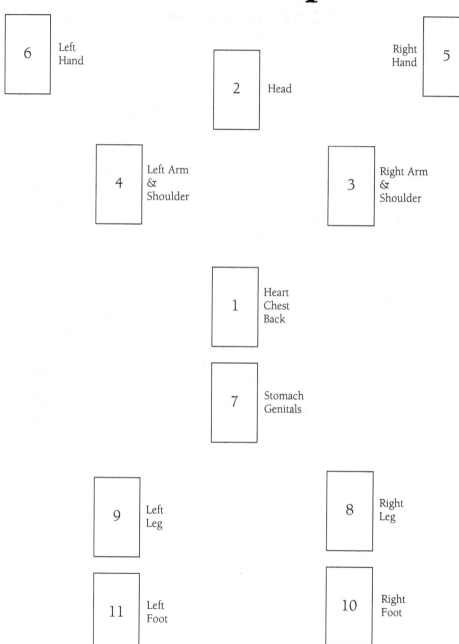

6 — Left Hand

2 — Head

5 — Right Hand

4 — Left Arm & Shoulder

3 — Right Arm & Shoulder

1 — Heart Chest Back

7 — Stomach Genitals

9 — Left Leg

8 — Right Leg

11 — Left Foot

10 — Right Foot

The Tree of Life Spread

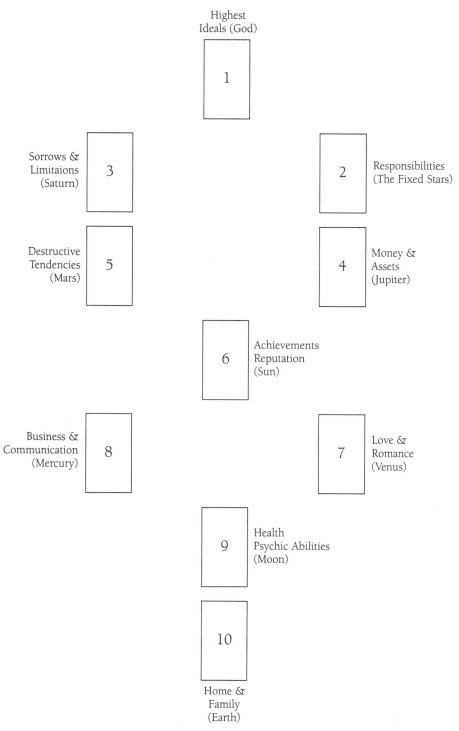

Highest
Ideals (God)

1

Sorrows &
Limitaions
(Saturn)

3

Responsibilities
(The Fixed Stars)

2

Destructive
Tendencies
(Mars)

5

Money &
Assets
(Jupiter)

4

Achievements
Reputation
(Sun)

6

Business &
Communication
(Mercury)

8

Love &
Romance
(Venus)

7

Health
Psychic Abilities
(Moon)

9

Home &
Family
(Earth)

10

The Pyramid Spread

			1			
		3		2		
	6		5		4	
10		9		8		7

15	14	13	12	11

21	20	19	18	17	16

28	27	26	25	24	23	23

*First Month	1			Seventh Month		14	15
Second Month	2	3		Eighth Month	16	17	18
Third Month	4	5		Ninth Month	19	20	
Fourth Month	6	7	8	Tenth Month	21	22	23
Fifth Month	9	10		Eleventh Month	24	25	26
Sixth Month	11	12	13	Twelfth Month		27	28

*This is given as an example. Either 2 or 3 cards will go with each month. It is up to you, the reader, to determine which card goes with which month.

The Three
3-Month Spread

1-4   First Month
5-8   Second Month
9-12 Third Month

Each card equals one week

4	3	2	1

8	7	6	5

12	11	10	9

Since it goes week by week, you may want to add a card to finish up the month you're in. For example, if you did this October 15th:

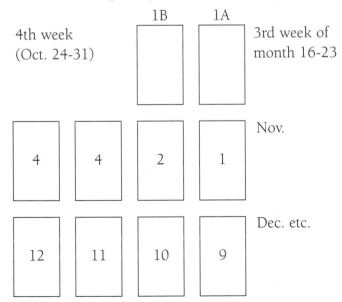

1B   1A

4th week   3rd week of
(Oct. 24-31)   month 16-23

4	4	2	1	Nov.

12	11	10	9	Dec. etc.

If the 8 of Wands was in position #2 it would mean a trip the 2nd week of November in the above example.

NUMBERS AND THE CARDS

Numerology is probably one of the oldest forms of divination—ever since man began to count and order things, he gave numbers special powers. Some were considered lucky, others (such as the number 13) are still looked upon unfavorably.

Odd numbers (1, 3, 5, 7, 9) are considered masculine or active. Even numbers (2, 4, 6, 8) are feminine or passive.

When an inordinate amount of one number comes up in a reading, that will especially emphasize the meaning of the number. Three or four aces show many new beginnings; three or four tens show that matters are being completed in several areas of life.

Here are the definitions of the numbers:

ZERO—The number 0 symbolizes the limitlessness light of creation, unbounded space and the primordial source. It contains nothingness and everything. The circular shape of the number has the properties of no beginning or end. Zero is called the number of God. It signifies the Fool of the Tarot.

ONE—The number 1 represents unity, the number of purpose, and new beginnings. It is characterized by action, ambition and aggression. It also represents the ego of a person and when multiplied by itself into infinity still remains the number one. Geometrically the Dot or Point is associated with the number 1, and it is associated with the Magician in the Major Arcana and the aces in the Minor Arcana.

TWO—The number 2 is the number of duality. It shows the two natures of things—good and bad, light and dark, Yin and Yang, joy and sorrow, etc. It stands for balance as well as contrast and maintains its equilibrium through a mixture of positive and negative qualities. It represents the unconscious mind of man. Geometrically the straight line connecting two points is associated with the number 2, as well as the High Priestess, Justice and the World in the Major Arcana and the twos of the Minor Arcana.

THREE—The number 3 shows versatility as symbolized by the triangle Δ. It combines talent with creativity making it the most adaptable of all numbers. It is the result of the combination of the first two numbers and therefore also represents completion of a cycle and the first geometric shape. Many people believe that "things happen in threes". It is associated with the Empress and the Hanged Man in the Major Arcana and the threes of the Minor Arcana.

FOUR—The number 4 is the number of steadiness and endurance, as represented by the square $\square$ geometrically. Its solidity is shown by the four points of a compass, the four seasons of the year and the four basic elements of earth, air, fire, and water. It stabilizes and builds a foundation. It is associated with the Emperor and Death in the Major Arcana and the fours of the Minor Arcana.

FIVE—The number 5 is the first of the spiritual odd numbers. It symbolizes adventure, experience, and uncertainty, and sometimes conflict. The Pentagram ☆ (five pointed star), represents man with his five extremities, (his head, 2 arms and 2 legs) and also his five senses. The four original elements plus ether or spirit add up to the number 5. It indicates expansion and instability. It is associated with the Hierophant and Temperance in the Major Arcana and the fives of the Minor Arcana.

SIX—The number 6 is a number of harmony and the higher vibration of the number 2. It represents dependability and service and is considered a perfect number, for when multiplying or adding together the first 3 prime numbers (1, 2, 3), 6 is the resulting figure. It is symbolized by the hexagram ✡ or Seal of Solomon. It is associated with beauty, marriage and labor. It resonates to the Lovers and the Devil in the Major Arcana and the sixes of the Minor Arcana.

SEVEN—The number 7 symbolizes mystery with study and knowledge as its way of exploring the unknown and the unseen. The ancients revered the number 7. It contains entire systems within it. In the Old Testament, God created heaven and earth in 6 days and rested on the 7th. There are seven ancient planets, seven days to the week and seven notes to the musical scale, along with seven ages of man, according to Shakespeare. It combines the unity of 1 and the perfection of 6. It is associated with the Chariot and the Tower in the Major Arcana and the sevens of the Minor Arcana.

EIGHT—The number 8 is the number of material success. It is a double cube, the higher octave of four. When halved it is equal (two 4s) and when halved again it is still equal (four 2s). Therefore it represents balance. Strength and the Star in the Major Arcana and the eights of the Minor Arcana are associated with this number.

NINE—The number 9 is the number of universal achievement and initiation. It is the last of the single digit numbers. As 3 times the number 3, the number 9 turns versatility into inspiration. It is a highly spiritual number. The Hermit is the end of the individual and the beginning of group consciousness. He is both the seeker of light and knowledge and the owner of information to dispense to others. The nines of the Minor Arcana contain wisdom also, as does the Moon, along with the Hermit in the Major Arcana.

TEN—The number 10 is the first of the 2 digit numbers and the climax to which the other numbers build. There are 10 cards to every suit in the Minor Arcana. It is the number 1 (ego and new beginnings) coupled with 0 (unbounded space). It is therefore a culmination of the previous 9 numbers and can be an exaggeration of the suit it represents. The Wheel of Fortune in the Major Arcana and the tens of the Minor Arcana are all inter-related with one another, as expressions of great changes and endings.

10 of Wands—extreme change—gain or release of a burden
10 of Cups—extreme happiness
10 of Swords—extreme difficulties
10 of Pentacles—extreme money

To find the basic numerical value of a number, you add up the digits (for example in the number 13, 1+3 = 4) to reduce it to a single digit. The Lovers and the Devil #6 and #15 both become 6 in this system. The High Priestess #2, Justice #11 and the World #20 all resonate to the same 2 vibration.

COLORS AND THE CARDS

Color is an intrinsic part of our lives. There have been studies conducted that clearly show the effect of a color on a person's moods—blue to be calming, red to grab one's attention (red stop lights and stop signs) and yellow to cheer a person up and stimulate energy. In the Tarot cards, colors are also influential in the meaning of the card. Bright blues and yellow backgrounds generally show much easier events than those cards with gray or black backgrounds. By just looking at the overall tone of the cards, through the colors that appear, you can get quite a bit of information.

Here is a list of colors and their meanings:

The color **RED** represents passion, earthly desire, action, and the need to use direction—also optimism, and cheerfulness.

The color **DARK RED** represents more violent or passionate emotions than a bright or clear red.

The color **PINK** represents less passionate, more loving emotions than bright red, since it is a combination of white and red.

The color **ORANGE** represents ambition. It is intelligence and earthly desires combined, because it is a blend of yellow and red.

The color **YELLOW** represents pure intelligence and/or scientific thought.

The color **YELLOW-BROWN** represents dullness or selfishness.

The color **BLUE** represents constancy of purpose; also strength and reliability.

The color **GREY-BLUE** represents uncertainty.

The color **GREEN** represents fertility and vegetation; also stability and healing.

The color **OLIVE GREEN** represents envy and cunning.

The color **PURPLE** represents spiritual endeavors, one who seeks mystic ideals, and/or has a highly developed imagination.

The color **BROWN** represents earthiness, practicality, plainness and honesty.

The color **REDDISH BROWN** represents sensuality.

The color **GREY** represents neutrality and/or uncertainty.

The color **BLACK** represents darkness, formality and convention. Since black is the absence of light it can symbolize ignorance and restrictions.

The color **WHITE** represents purity and the abstract thought of love.

SYMBOLS IN THE CARDS

The following is a list of Major Arcana cards and the Symbols in each of them and what those symbols represent. As symbols, they of course are not bound to a particular card—a wand represents will power whether the Fool carries it on his shoulder or whether the Hermit leans upon a full-sized staff (or wand). When a symbol is used in more than one card, (for example the infinity sign over the Magician and the Woman in the Strength card), the definition will be under the earlier numbered card.

These definitions are suggestions—a certain symbol may mean something different to you.

THE FOOL—The Wand the Fool carries represents will power, determination and direction.

The Purse he carries represents universal memory and instinct.

The Eagle on the purse represents a symbol of height, of the spirit of the Sun, and strength.

The White Rose represents purity.

The White Dog has evolved from a wolf to a domesticated animal through nature and symbolizes evolution. It also is a symbol of faithfulness.

The Mountain represents loftiness of nature, and also spirituality.

The Feather represents the wind, air, and freedom.

THE MAGICIAN—The Cosmic Lemniscate represents eternal life and is the symbol of infinity ∞.

The Snake devouring its own tail is called an ouroboros and is another symbol for eternity, and the continuity of life.

The Red Roses represent the emotion of desire.

The White Lilies represent abstract thought.

THE HIGH PRIESTESS—The B on the pillar stands for the Hebrew word BOAZ which can be translated as severity.

The J on the pillar stands for the Hebrew word JACHIN which can be translated as mercy.

The Solar Cross represents a balance of positive and negative forces.

The Pomegranates represent the female life force.

The Palm Leaves represent the male life force.

The bottom of the Gown represents the stream of the unconscious mind.

The Crown on the High Priestess is made up of a full moon and two crescent moons (one waxing and one waning) and is also called the crown of Hathor, who was an Egyptian Goddess.

THE EMPRESS— ♀ is the symbol of Venus on her shield.

The Myrtle Leaves shown were sacred to Venus, as were the Pearls on her neck.

The Scepter represents power and authority.

The Wheat represents fertility.

The Stream of Water represents the unconscious mind.

The Twelve Stars represent the twelve signs of the Zodiac.

THE EMPEROR—The Rams Heads were sacred to Mars.

The Ankh was the Egyptian symbol of life.

The Globe in his hand represents dominion and power over others.

The Mountains represent reality.

THE HIEROPHANT—The Crossed Keys represent solar and lunar energy.

The Triple Crown is divided into three parts: the lower part is the material world; the middle part is the formative world; the top part is the creative world.

The Triple Staff represents body, mind and soul.

THE LOVERS—The Archangel Raphel is the Archangel of air and represents the superconscious mind.

The Man represents the conscious mind.

The Woman represents the subconscious mind.

The twelve leaves in the tree behind the man represent the 12 signs of the Zodiac.

THE CHARIOT—The Eight Pointed Star represents dominion.

The Square on his chest represents physical reality.

The Canopy of Stars shows celestial influences.

The Wings on the chariot represent inspiration.

The Hindu Sign of positive and negative or male and female forces, ⚢ is called a yoni.

The two Sphinxes correspond to the two pillars of the High Priestess, one black, one white, and represent mystery.

The Symbols on the Charioter's skirt are alchemical symbols.

STRENGTH—The Lion represents the animal or lower instincts of man.

The Flowers on the woman represent growth and fertility.

The White Gown represents purity and spirituality.

THE HERMIT—The Lantern represents the light of truth.

The Staff represents power and control.

The Snow of the mountain represents cold reality and abstract thought.

WHEEL OF FORTUNE—Typhon (the snake) was the force which devoured the world in Egyptian mythology and also represents the life force.

Hermes-Anubis, the jackel headed God represents intelligence.

The Sphinx represents mystery and hidden knowledge.

The four Hebrew Letters יהוה represented the name of God which was never spoken. (The ancients believed that to speak the name of a god gave you power over it.) It is translated as YOD HE VAU HE and called the tetragrammaton (4 letters).

The letters T-A-R-O on the wheel are an anagram which spell Tarot, or Rota (wheel) or Orat (to speak), or Tora (the law), or Ator (the Goddess Hathor). The sentence would read "The Wheel of the Tarot speaks the Law of Hathor."

The four symbols in the wheel are mercury, salt, sulphur and water.

The four Winged Figures can represent the four Apostles of the Bible or the four fixed signs of the Zodiac.

JUSTICE—The Circle in the Square ⧇ represents spirituality (the circle) contained within physical reality (the square).

The Scales represent balance and justice.

The Veil between the pillars shows that the figure of Justice guards some hidden knowledge, perhaps hidden from mortal man.

THE HANGED MAN—The Leaves represent growth and fertility.

His Crossed Legs form an inverted 4 (ㄣ). 4 is the number of earth, reversed it is spirit.

His Head and Arms form a triangle, representing creativity and spirituality.

He is made up of the Three Primary Colors—red, blue and yellow—showing how basic this card is to everyone (transformation and spirituality).

DEATH—The Sun Rising represents a new beginning.

The White Rose represents the life force.

The River in the background is the river Styx that the Greeks believed led to the underworld.

The King (representing secular power) is lying down, but the Priest (representing spiritual power) is standing.

The Priest's Staff which represents his worldly power is lying on the ground.

TEMPERANCE—Michael is the Archangel of Fire and represents the sun, as shown by the solar disc on his forehead.

The Iris Flowers were sacred to the sun.

The Crown in the background represents mastery and attainment.

Michael has one foot in Water and one foot on Land, representing a balance between his conscious and unconscious mind.

There is a Triangle within a Square on Michael's chest. The $\triangle$ represents spirit, the $\square$ is matter.

THE DEVIL—The Donkey Ears represent stubbornness.

He has Bat Wings, Donkey Ears, Goat Legs and Horns, and Bird Feet, and is composed of different animals. These combine to show his animalistic, instinctive nature.

⛧—the inverted Pentagram points down to earth as does the torch he holds (the earth represents the material plane).

♄ —on his right hand palm is the sign of Saturn.

The Chains represent servitude, bondage, and restriction.

THE TOWER—The Lightning represents inspiration and great power.

ᛉ —The Hebrew letter Yod represents the life force.

The Crown represents mastery and attainment.

THE STAR—The 8 Pointed Star represents power and material success.

The Five Riverlets represent the five senses.

The Seven Stars represent the seven main chakra points of the body or the seven ancient planets.

The Bird in the tree is an Ibis, a bird sacred to the ancient Egyptians.

The Water is the unconscious mind and emotions, which are being poured into water (unconscious mind) and land (the conscious mind).

THE MOON—The Dog represents an animal that is tamed or domesticated.

The Wolf symbolizes a more primitive and wild animal nature, and the Crayfish is even more primordial and primitive. The crayfish would be the unconscious mind of man, the wolf the conscious and the dog would be the superconscious.

The ❥ s are the same as in the Tower—Yods—life energy/forces.

THE SUN—The Sun itself is a symbol of light and warmth (all life on earth is dependent on the sun).

The Wall represents a division between spaces; the child on a horse is in front of the wall; he is beyond a limiting situation as symbolized by the wall.

The Sunflower was sacred to the sun. The 4 sunflowers represent the four elements.

The 21 rays of the sun are symbolic of the 21 Major Arcana cards with the center representing the Fool.

JUDGEMENT—The Archangel is Gabriel, the Archangel of water (spirit and emotions).

The Coffins float on water (the subconscious mind) and represents an awakening, as the people (the physical bodies) are standing to hear the angel (the spiritual message).

The Red Solar Cross on the flag corresponds to the sun.

THE WORLD—The 4 Fixed Signs of the Zodiac are in the corners. They are the Lion—Leo, the Bull—Taurus, the Man—Aquarius and the Eagle—higher side of Scorpio.

The Double-Edged Wands represent power and control.

The Wreath or garland represents unity and eternity (being formed in the shape of a circle.)

The Woman's Legs form a cross or a number 4 with her arms and head forming a triangle, representing spirit over matter ♀, the ultimate triumph.

ON KEEPING A TAROT JOURNAL

One of the most effective ways I've found for people to get more in touch with their Tarot cards is to keep a Tarot Journal.

To keep a Tarot Journal one must shuffle the deck at night, pull 3 cards and place them face down, from right to left. The cards are left in that position until the next evening, when they are then turned face up and studied. The reason you don't look at the cards before-hand is that you don't want to influence your expectations for the day. And if they are difficult cards, you might be upset without cause.

Card #1 represents the events of the morning. Card #2 represents the afternoon, and Card #3 shows the evening's events. By studying what cards come up and reviewing the day's events, you can see a connection to the card, and perhaps gain some meanings that will be yours alone to associate with that card.

For example, one evening, on looking at the day's cards, I had the 4 of Swords for the morning card, the Sun card in the afternoon, and the Knight of Pentacles in the evening.

That day I awoke very sick and had to spend the morning in bed. (The 4 of Swords can be meditating and resting.) In the afternoon I received a phone call from a friend I had not talked to in at least a year! (The Sun represents happy feelings, and is in my opinion the card in the deck that offsets negative cards.) I also was starting to feel much better in the afternoon. That evening a dark haired man with brown eyes dropped over to see me—the Knight of Pentacles (no, he wasn't my knight in shining armor, only a friend). By these examples you can see that the practice of associating the 78 cards with actual events in your life can go a long way towards getting the cards to communicate to you, and will make you a more effective and accurate reader.

SOME THOUGHTS ON THE CARDS

Yes, the court cards are the most difficult to read. First of all, they represent people, and people are so different. (Is his hair dark or medium brown? Are her eyes hazel or light brown? What if he's blond haired with brown eyes? Where's the bald-headed man's card? etc.) Also, the Waite deck is sexist—there are not as many women as men. It's also racist—there are no Blacks, Orientals, Hispanics, etc. In spite of these shortcomings, I find the symbols of this deck to be clearly and simply drawn and I like Pamela Coleman Smith's art work. As a reader, you must adjust the cards to the person. In reading for a gay man, for example, the Queen of Pentacles might represent a dark haired man in his circle of friends, instead of a dark haired woman. Get the idea? It all can get confusing, but follow your intuition.

Next, in regards to romance, it's unfortunate that the most asked about subject is the least accurate to diagnose with the cards. My feeling is that to be truly accurate, both people involved in the relationship would have to have their cards read. Then, comparing both spreads a more accurate portrait is obtained. This is not always easy to do because usually one person in a relationship is more open to getting a reading and may be more obsessed with the relationship.

We also still have free will—that's the bottom line. I say that when I read the cards, usually what comes up will occur, but the events are not carved in stone. Unpleasant circumstances can be avoided and good things can be delayed or not happen at all due to the person's free will.

So what's the purpose of a reading? Well, many times a reading will confirm for someone things they already know at a more subconscious level. Or a reading may present a new way to look at a situation. Sometimes a reading will give a person the shot of confidence needed to carry through an idea or plan. And sometimes a reading is just plain fun!

As long as people are curious about their future, there will exist Tarot cards and people who who read them.

And after studying this book, you are now one of them! Welcome!

BIOGRAPHICAL NOTES

Janet Berres has been studying, reading and teaching the Tarot for over 24 years, but has been interested in a wide range of metaphysics her whole life (and probably past lives too!). She is a member of MENSA and of NCGR (National Council for Geocosmic Research), an astrological organization. She has taught at Northwestern University in Evanston, IL, Triton College in River Grove, IL and Northeastern University in Chicago, IL, all for their adult education programs. She is also a reader in private practice and has earned her livelihood through her Tarot skills for over 20 years, while raising her two sons. She is founding Mother and President of the International Tarot Society.

You can contact the author by writing her at:
P.O. Box 1475
Morton Grove, IL 60053

NOTES